CW00494232

Crea

First published in Great Britain, 2023 by C H Press, a division of Creative Hats.

First published in hardback in Hertfordshire in 2023 by C H Books, an imprint of Creative Hats.

This paperback edition published in 2023.

Cover design by: Tom McManus, C H Books

Edited by: Tom McManus, Creative Hats

Tom McManus

About the author

I am a passionate believer in the purpose and value of education, having taught in every environment from a university to a prison. I have seen first-hand the advantages that come with embracing education, and the limitations that can come with a lack of education.

A degree is something to which more and more people are aspiring, and it opens doors that nothing else can. However wealthy you are, you cannot practice medicine without a medical degree!! The same is true of many professions and careers.

My aim in writing this book is to help you make the most of your time at university. You are building the foundation of the life that lies ahead of you. My hope for you is that you achieve everything you dream of, and wish for

By the same author:

"Stand out as a Graduate"

https://www.the**openingdoorsprogramme**.com
https://www.facebook.com/OpeningDoorsProgramme/
https://www.instagram.com/openingdoorsprogramme/
https://twitter.com/OpeningDP

Your University Journey

Living, Learning and Growing

Dedication

Written with the help of Michael, Kelly and many other graduates who gave their time generously. They have shared their experiences and memories to help you prepare for yours and create your own memories.

Dean Taylor was a great collaborator, and his input was very valuable.

Contents

Introduction

I am a great believer in the value and importance of human potential, and seeing it realised is wonderful. Realising and maximising your potential is the key to a worthwhile and fulfilling life and career.

The world of work is constantly changing. Technology and machines have replaced people in many industries, and resulted in a global change in working patterns. A generation ago we had hundreds of factories in the UK, employing millions of workers. Now a generation of people must compete with each other for highly skilled jobs. We have thousands of social influencers, but no bus conductors or lift operators anymore.

When employers advertise for graduate applicants, differentiating yourself from your peers becomes harder. This book is aimed at showing you how, starting before you even leave for university, to make the most of your time there, and put yourself in a great position to find and pursue your chosen career path when the time comes.

Make the most of your time at university, but please remember, it is a journey, not a joyride. This book does not contain any guarantees, or magic formulae. It is not a panacea. It is intended solely to raise awareness of certain topics and encourage forethought, planning and reflection. It highlights some key points and milestones on your student journey.

Point to ponder

Take the time to ask people you know have graduated if they could tell you one thing they would change, if they could go back.

"I wish I had…………"

"I wish I hadn't………"

Make a note of what they say. It will be a good guide for you, going forward.

Preparing to get ready

We want you to stay safe, do well and have fun!

Normally, getting ready is a straightforward process that doesn't take a great deal of time. We may be getting ready to go to school, to go out for the evening, to go on holiday, or perhaps to take a test or sit an examination. Getting ready is something you do on the day, or maybe the day before.

Never before have you needed to get ready to change every part of every day of your life!! This is where preparation plays a very large part. We usually have some sort of checklist in our head that ensures we don't miss a step. When you're changing your life, no such list exists. Therefore, making one is the first step in your preparation.

Start by looking in every room at home. This will tell you what you will need to take with you. Things you have at home found just by looking won't be there at university. Use this to list what you will need.

A colleague who is ex-military tells me that the Army give troops two instructions prior to any movement:

1. Prepare to move
2. Move

A good way to organise your move to university. As with soldiers, you are not planning to return in the near future, so you have to take what you will need when you reach your destination. In your case, the halls of residence.

Buy early!! When you get to university you will struggle to buy such things as a kettle, a toaster, bedding, or towels at a good price. You will pay a lot more than you need to, and you may not even find certain things at all. You are not the only person starting life at university, and there are only so many kettles in the world!!

Learn how to shop. Aldi and Lidl are set up in almost every university town. Sandwich and pie shops sell stock cheaply late in the day. Go round a supermarket before you leave home to familiarise yourself with the process of shopping if you haven't done it before.

Links are not recommendations

Students - ALDI UK

Up to 10% OFF | Aldi Student Discount | August 2021 (hotdeals.com)

Be sure that, if you arrive at your halls of residence, possibly hundreds of miles from home, and you've forgotten something, you're either doing without it or buying a replacement. Incidentally, you have no idea where the shops are, so that's the second problem.

Point to ponder:

Intentions do not get anything done - action does!!

The adventure begins.

You are now living the first great adventure of your life!! All the constraints and control measures from home have been shaken off. You are as free as a bird!!

Now that you are free, your freedom allows you to make mistakes. Uncorrected and unnecessary mistakes can have serious, and sometimes tragic, consequences. The control measures and constraints you may have resented at home have kept you safe.

The temptation to try things simply because you weren't allowed to try them at home should be resisted. There is a very good reason your family did not want/allow you to do certain things.

Learning from your mistakes is a natural part of personal development, going back to the earliest days of human existence.

Learning from your mistakes takes times and means learning the hard way. Learning from other people's mistakes is learning the easy way. This is the value of families. You see constraints and control; your family see a safety net. So will you if you look!!

Take a few moments to search the links. Real insights from people who have already made the journey you are embarking on.

Things I wish I'd known before going to university.

Every Graduate and Postgraduate student will have their version of things they wish they'd known in advance. In time you will perhaps have some insights of your own!! The purpose of this chapter is to highlight examples that will make your transition and university journey, easier, better and more fulfilling.

Real insights from graduates who have already made the journey you are embarking on. Take a few moments to search the links.

Things I Wish I'd Known Before I Went To Uni - Student bloggers - Cardiff University

"Lecturers are there to talk to. They really don't want you to fail their module. Honestly, if you're struggling, you should definitely talk to them. If you like their module, talk to them. If you want to know more about your module, or if there's more that you can do, or if you'd like book recommendations- pretty much anything really - ask your lecturer! Obviously they have their own work to do, but they'll be happy to talk to you at some point about their research."

Things I wish I'd known before coming to university... | Royal Agricultural University (rau.ac.uk)

"Freshers' doesn't have to be the best week of your life – There's a common misconception that Freshers' week will be one of the best weeks of your life, however this might not always be the case. You might feel pressure to settle in, find friends quickly, know your way around campus, join loads of clubs and have the best time socialising ever night. The purpose of Freshers' week is to give you opportunities to socialise to start the friend making process. However, it is reasonable to say no to things and be homesick. On a personal note, I was so homesick during Freshers' that I cried every day. And when I tell others that I did, they said they felt the same. Homesickness is a normal thing and the good thing about the RAU is that they have support systems in place where you can go and talk to someone about it."

Things I wish I'd known before uni | University of Suffolk (uos.ac.uk)

Get yourself a schedule.

"Uni gives you so much free time and it's tempting to use that to go shopping or binge on your favourite Netflix shows. Get yourself into a habit of setting times for socialising, study and exercise so that you're not drowning in work halfway through the semester."

Things I Wish I'd Known Before I Went To Uni - Student bloggers - Cardiff University

Point to ponder:

"T(t)he ability/appetite to learn from others is rather found unequally distributed amongst us, and it is argued that those who are able to learn from other's experiences much more are at an advantage when it comes to overcoming problems in personal, social & professional lives."

Source: 7 Benefits of learning from someone else's experiences (headstrt.com)

Here we are at last,

it's fresher's week!!

Things you would never dream of doing at home suddenly seem attractive and exciting. Hang on though, there's a reason you didn't do them at home!!

The Swedish student, 28, killed after he was 'catapulted' from a shopping trolley travelling at 80km/h - as police says his injured friend riding on the back 'could face charges' | Daily Mail Online

This video shows you why you should never ride a shopping trolley down a flight of stairs - Mirror Online

Freshers' week survival guide | Drinkaware

How to stay safe this freshers' week - Unifresher

There is a reason we don't allow people to drive cars at any speed they choose. First of all, it's incredibly dangerous, and secondly, people constantly overestimate their own ability to do things. One may be their ability to drive.

The Dunning–Kruger effect is a cognitive bias whereby people with low ability, expertise, or experience regarding a certain type of a task or area of knowledge tend to overestimate their ability or knowledge. Some researchers also include in their definition the opposite effect for high performers: their tendency to underestimate their skills.

Being confident nothing will happen is not a guarantee you will stay safe. People choose to believe it. Early man had an instinct for survival, and we are here because it worked!! Dangerous things are called dangerous for a reason!!

Be aware of risks and dangers, often posed by other people who don't stick to the rules. A driving instructor in the USA once gave a piece of advice which fits perfectly here. He was talking about being aware that other people can and do break the rules of the road.

"You can have right of way and still be dead."

Why are you here?

"I'm going to Uni".

Many, many people, say that now. It is almost a default setting for students leaving school.

You're finally here. Fresher's week is behind you. The dust has settled. Lectures are starting tomorrow. Now it's real. You are a student. Question; why are you at university??

Some popular answers include:

- To have some fun

- To be independent

- To make new friends

- To live the dream

Many other answers are possible.

There is one other answer to think about. What was it??... ....oh yes, to get a degree!!

Point to ponder:

According to Dean Taylor, one of the keys to succeeding at university is to treat it is a full-time job.

PS: He really knows what he's talking about!

Your primary purpose is/should be to obtain the best degree you possibly can.

When you talk about your university journey at some time in the future, don't say; "I could/should have done better, I could/should have worked harder." It's too late then. Seize the opportunity.

The other reasons you give for going can be achieved elsewhere, by doing other things. You need to be at university to get your degree, so take it seriously.

More will be said about advice later in this book, but it's relevant here as well. You will be advised by other freshers, and you may choose to ask them for advice. They do not know more about university life than you do, they really don't!! They may have older siblings, parents, or grandparents who have been to university, but that does not matter.

In order to understand your situation, others who would advise you would need to be with you now, sharing their experience/advice with you. The best your fellow, super confident freshers can do, is guess or assume, based on what they think or believe. Neither is any good to you, but believing your fellow freshers can send you down a path you should not take. The only advice you should take should be provided by experts, and be paid for.

You're paying for your time at university, and there are many experts, in several disciplines, only a click away!! I'm not suggesting for one moment you should be unfriendly or dismissive in any way. You'll all be living and working in close proximity, and tension is certainly unhelpful. Think about advice people who no more than you are giving, and consider it in those terms. Opinions and expert advice are two different things entirely.

You are the author of the book that tells your life story, and, when you write the ending to this chapter, make sure it's the happiest ending possible. **Your dream came true, because you made it come true.**

Point to ponder:

Hell is the truth seen too late!!

Getting there and back

You will acquaint yourself with the campus fairly quickly and learn the geography of the local area within a few days. You will be orientated and confident before you know it.

On a night out there is a different situation to consider. First of all, darkness is disorientating. Secondly, alcohol is not your friend, it really isn't!! You need to get back to your halls safely. Taxis are a great way to get around, they are convenient and comfortable. When you go out, you need to get back safely and without incident.

Ionically, the driver doesn't know the campus as well as you. He/she has been driving a taxi in the town for twenty years and knows every street. They will never get lost. The universities are dynamic institutions. They regularly add new buildings, rename buildings, and demolish buildings.

This means things changes significantly. The taxi drivers won't know what all the changes are, why would they?

We now live in a world that is incredibly interconnected. Google, Amazon, Deliveroo, and others have changed how we live, work, and shop. This is also true of travel. Uber has become a byword for taxi. Scenario; you and some friends have been out for the evening. It's time to get back, and a taxi is the way to go. Safe, quick and convenient. Should you have an Uber account, you will be very popular, but also quite a lot poorer quite quickly. It will be very hard to collect a share of the fare from your fellow travellers. Having that discussion before you get into the taxi will not be good idea. Be fair to others, and pay your fair share of what is due when you're out together, but remember that's a two way street.

Therefore, your best way to help its to pick an established landmark very near your halls, that the taxi driver will know. Pubs, cinemas, public buildings are examples of places they will know.

Choose one, and they will be able to find it. All you then need to do is to provide details of the last part of the journey.

Points to ponder:

The first person who should take responsibility for your safety is you.

It's been said for a very long time; it's true today, and will be true for as long as humans live together;

a fool and his money are soon parted.

It's just like school, isn't it?

Up to this point, your only understanding of the education system has been based on your time at school. Let's do a quick compare and contrast; what's the same and what's different?

A school and a university are both places of education, and both have large numbers of students. After that, we're already on to contrasting; things that are different.

What cannot, ever, be in dispute, is that your degree studies add another level to the complexity of any work you have done at school. In addition to reflecting your understanding of the subject and your test readiness, it also reflects your level of planning, dedication and determination. At this point it is well worth noting that future employers also know this.

It is a mistake to assume that a university is a school without a bell. You are taking ownership of your education, and with it, ownership of your results and your future direction of travel.

We all seem to know at least one person who is lazy but very bright. They don't do much work in school, they coast along. Then, come examination time, they do very well. The school system suits this person perfectly. The result achieved is based on understanding of the subject matter, and the way you perform on the day.

Universities don't work in the same way, and it would be a huge mistake to think or believe that they do. During your university journey, you will submit many pieces of work for marking. Every piece of work you submit is significant. It is the equivalent of every piece of homework you submitted at school being used to help decide your grade in a subject. What this means is you cannot have a day off. You cannot submit a poor or indifferent piece of work without it impacting on the eventual outcome.

Not all your work is graded in the same way. You need to check with your lecturers to ensure you know exactly what each piece of work is worth. It will vary from institution to institution, and indeed, from subject to subject.

It is quite possible that, before you have even completed your second year, you have limited your eventual grade/classification. Your work is aggregated, which means you have not achieved the level required to get the grade you wanted. You will, undoubtedly, be awarded the grade your work deserves. By the time you reach this realisation, it may well be too late!! We will explore this in more detail in the next chapter.

When you choose not to attend lectures, alarm bells will not ring. Schools set a process in motion the instant a student does not attend. Universities don't work in quite the same way. You are literally wasting your own time and money when you don't attend. Do you imagine when you enter the world of work any employer would accept you turning up only when you felt like it? The difference is that they are paying you; at university you are the one paying.

You will almost certainly be able to access recordings of lectures using YouTube or a similar platform. However, you can't interact with the video, and you can't ask it questions. There is a huge value to attending lectures. It is said that in life, showing up is half the battle. When you do, you are prime position to make the most of the investment of your time.

Points to ponder:

- Submit your best work, first time, every time!! Check regularly to ensure you are on course to achieve your personal goal.
- Do all your university work as well as you can, when you supposed to, every time. Do it right or do it twice. This option costs you marks!!
- There are two days every week when you cannot do any work: yesterday and tomorrow.

Your first year; does it really matter?

Much has been said and written about this. Let's look at it in more detail. Let's look at this from both inside the university, and from outside.

- ## Inside the university
  ### At this point, everything is within your control.

During your first year you are doing things you have never done before. You're living away from home, coping with a level of academic challenge which is new, and making all manner of adjustments to many areas of your personal life. It is a combination of achievements and challenges.

The more demanding work will be starting in your second year. During your first year you will have found out more about your preferred learning style and how to structure and present your work. It has probably been the first time you have used complex referencing systems and had to meet hard deadlines. Overall, it's something of a roller coaster ride.

That said, there are standards to be met. It will change from university to university, but you must attain a minimum mark or percentage required by the institution before you move to the second year. Unless this is achieved, you may find yourself having to repeat your first year. Consequently, a three-year degree takes four years to compete. There are other options.

- You may be offered the chance to re-sit before the new academic year.
- You may be offered the chance to change your degree,
- You may be offered the chance or to retake failed modules next year. This is similar to retaking an AS module you failed during your second year of A Levels, when you are taking A2 levels.

The university will do everything possible to help you move forward, but you can avoid this situation ever becoming a reality by taking your first year seriously, and doing what you need to do, as well as you can do it, when you need to do it. With this in mind, we now take a look at something upon which your university journey, and eventual degree classification will hinge.

Your assignment is due today!! Once upon a time, when things were simpler, you rushed to the door just before the deadline and pushed the envelope under it. Made it!!

Today you click "send" just in time!!

On this particular occasion, you know for sure that the work you're submitting is sub-standard, but you can't miss the deadline. When it comes back with corrections required, you can resubmit, and you'll get top marks.

Only half right, unfortunately.

In most circumstances you will be allowed to resubmit. It is dangerous to actually assume this. However, any assumption you make about your mark is misplaced. When work is resubmitted, you should assume the best mark you can achieve is a pass, regardless of the quality of the work.

Lecturers do not want to mark work twice; it literally doubles their workload.

You could have submitted that quality of work first time around, but you didn't. You chose not to. You weren't left with no other choice, it was your decision. It's on you!!

Going forward, this will ultimately impact your grade and classification. You made a choice to wait until the last minute, then try to buy more time by submitting work you know would bounce back. Ask yourself how you would feel if you were the lecturer. Students want you to do twice as much work because they didn't want to do the work when you asked them to do it. You did agree a deadline with them, so lecturers can't be criticised. The message you are sending lecturers when you behave like this is; "let me have another go, I'll take it seriously this time."

Really??

• Outside the university

At this point, nothing is within your control.

You have obtained your degree and you are now job hunting. You are presenting your CV with a great covering e-mail, and you're being interviewed for your dream job. Suddenly, your first year comes back to bite you, hard!!

The interviewers ask to see your transcript. This is the story of your degree journey, warts and all. It shows everything, including your first-year performance. They may well conclude you did not take your time at university as seriously as you could/should have, therefore, offering someone with such a casual attitude a large salary and bonuses may not represent a good investment. You appear not to have taken your time at university seriously, would you take their job role seriously?

Should the interviewer take such a gamble when they have a list of other candidates to interview? You will never know for sure. The interviewers are most unlikely to give unsuccessful candidates any feedback on the interview. Why would they? They're busy people, and there is nothing to be gained by wasting time telling an unsuccessful candidate why they didn't get the job.

Let's assume you decide to find a job during your time at university. You're working in a fast-food outlet, serving customers. Every order you take is wrong, and has to be replaced, free of charge. The job didn't last long!! You then find a job working behind the bar in a local pub. Every drink you serve is wrong, and has to be replaced, free of charge. Again, the job didn't last long.

When we do a job badly, we have to do it again, and that takes time and/or money. This is true of every piece of work you submit at university. When it is below the standard you know you should reach, it either comes back, and costs you more time to do it again, and results in serious time pressure as the end of your course looms, or it obtains just enough marks for a pass.

You have therefore made a decision to limit the extent to which you can succeed, because you wouldn't take the time necessary to meet the standard. It isn't vitally important to you that you get the orders right in the jobs we described, you can learn from your mistakes and find another job. Not true with university. When your work is less than it should/could be, it costs you, in the short, medium and long term.

Why would you pay for your education and then not make every effort to do as well as possible? Incidentally, don't take any notice of what your fellow students tell you about their own work. You know what is required of you, so don't be led by someone telling you to take your foot of the pedal and go out for the evening instead of working.

You are missing lectures and submitting sub-standard work at the last second. You are paying thousands of pounds every year for this opportunity, but you're choosing to waste both time and money, as well as limiting the chances of obtaining the best possible result. It is the equivalent of booking a table in a restaurant, arriving late, not ordering any food, paying what the meal you would have ordered costs, and then leaving. You're a generous person, so you probably left a nice tip as well!!

Unlike school, content alone is not enough. Your work must be presented in the manner required by the university. Failure to do so will cost you marks, and can, ultimately, result in your degree being less than you anticipated. Learning how to present work is of critical importance. Obtain detailed guidance. Find out if templates or examples are available. Referencing is a skill in itself. Learn how to do it. There is more than one system for referencing, make certain you know how to do it. The quality of your assignment, and the mark you receive, is measured by every word you write, and by how it is presented.

"Cramming" is a popular word in university circles, but as a strategy it is a nonstarter. Returning briefly to school, it was possible to cram for a test or exam and be rewarded for your efforts with an excellent mark or grade. It is a single piece of work, marked and measured in isolation. University is different. Every piece of work is important, so cramming will impact only on one piece of work. It will not influence the final outcome. It's a full-time job, so you shouldn't have to do such a thing.

The UK university grading system explained.

The UK university grading system explained (greatbritishmag.co.uk)

How Do University Credits Work? - Student's Guide (thinkstudent.co.uk)

"There is a clear distinction between the grades as achieving 70% and above requires a significant level of both knowledge and understanding of your subject, as well as the willingness to go beyond the scope of what you are taught, do extra reading and see things from a different and new perspective."

Points to ponder:

You're at university. Submit your best possible work first time. You are paying thousands of pounds for every year you are there. Why would you not submit your best work. You're only cheating yourself out of the marks you deserve.

It is often said life is not a rehearsal, and it is undoubtedly true. When we make a mistake or an error, we recognise it and correct it. The shorter the time taken to recognise a mistake, and the shorter the time taken to correct it, the better. Think about this in terms of your time at university.

When we get lost, we can retrace our steps quickly. Spending three years at university, then realising that you should have worked harder and been more committed, is not the same. Youn cannot rewind and start again. Be able to say; "I did as well as I could." You owe it to yourself, and your future self.

Planning isn't everything

Planning is critical to success in almost every area of our lives. Some things happen as a result of an impulsive act, such as suddenly deciding to buy a lottery ticket and becoming an instant millionaire. This is not going to be the case with your time at university. However, we are saying planning isn't everything, so surely, the title of this chapter is wrong. No, it isn't!!

The only time a plan is of any use whatsoever is when it is executed. This is where it can all fall down. We devise and design a brilliant plan, commit it to paper, or save it to our desktop. Perhaps we can see it on our mobile phone every day.

This is specific to your work, not to your personal or social life.

Some key changes include:

- You will be working at a level you have never worked at before.
- You will be working independently.
- You will be writing in an academic style.
- You will not be chased for late work. It is your responsibility to submit it.

Every January millions of people say they are going to lose weight and get fit.

Part one of the plan.

They choose a gym.

Part two of the plan.

They decide on the right type of membership, based on what they want to achieve and their own levels of athleticism.

Part three of the plan.

They decide what days/times they are able to visit the gym each week.

Part four of the plan.

They sign up for the membership they have chosen.

Part five of the plan.

They set up the direct debit to make their payment each month.

Part six of the plan.

They buy the clothing and equipment they need. They spend what they feel they need to spend. This is going to be life changing!!

Part seven of the plan.

They buy some books on healthy eating. Amazon is great for that sort of thing!!

Part eight of the plan.

They tell their friends what they have decided to do.

Part nine of the plan.

They Programme their electronic planner/mobile to ensure they do not double book themselves.

Part ten of the plan.

They have to get out of the chair, get in the car, and go to the gym, regardless of the weather!!

At what point does the plan fail? When does it all go for nothing?

When we reach the "do" part!!

Point to ponder:

You can fool most of the people most of the time, but you can't fool yourself for a single second.

I'll start next week for sure, honest I will!!

This is where the plan often falls apart. These millions of people check their bank statement every month and see that the money has left their account. Then they pick the most credible/ least incredible excuse or not going and order a takeaway instead.

That is the so often the human condition. It is said the spirit is willing, but the flesh is weak. We fall down at the point of execution. **It's great to plan, but ultimately worthless until you actually have to do something apart from planning.**

This is true of your time at university. You can have detailed, multi-layered plans on a spreadsheet, with events/dates highlighted. It is there as a reminder of what you promised yourself you would do.

Give yourself the best chance of success: plan your work, then work your plan!

6 best student planner apps | Calendly.com

"The most common commodity in this country is unrealised potential".

Calvin Coolidge

Point to ponder:

To repeat the advice from Dean Taylor, consider your life as a student to be a full-time job. 9-5 is a familiar expression. It does not have to be literally 9-5, but you pick the hour's best suited to your psychology and learning style. Night owls work better at different times to early birds.

Money makes your student world go round

Student bank accounts is a highly competitive market. Not all accounts are the same. The bank you choose may well be the bank you stay with for your working life. This is why they work so hard to win you as a customer in the first place.

Ways to make the process easier.

- Arrange it before you leave home.
- Ask someone who has experience to help you choose.

Make a note to self: Overdrafts cost money!!

Links are not recommendations.

Student bank accounts 2021: Overdraft limits and perks on offer (inews.co.uk)

Remember money, or more specifically, the lack of it, has a huge effect on you psychological wellbeing. You cannot concentrate properly when you are stressed. Financial problems are well known to be serious stressors. It will impact on every part of your life.

Start by calculating how much money you have, and decide what your spending priorities are. What is essential, and what is not. Convenience is not a consideration. Understand that if you can save money, it will benefit you. A simple spreadsheet will help. Never assume you should try to match other people when it comes to spending. You have no idea what their circumstances are.

Links are not recommendations

- Student Budgeting Planner - incl. spreadsheets to help you budget - MSE (moneysavingexpert.com)

- https://www.bing.com/search?q=student+bud geting+spreadsheet&cvid=11d1b0819b844a208 d81fab4091174de&aqs=edge.3.69i57j0l6.1752 3j0j1&pglt=43&FORM=ANNTA1&PC=DCTS

The ATM is a source of cold hard facts. It won't dispense cash just because you want it to. We all sometimes wish it would!! They're never wrong. Banks are better at controlling and managing money than you are, including yours. Entering your PIN then crossing your fingers and offering up a silent prayer won't make it dispense cash.

When you find yourself, quite literally penniless, the impact on your mental and physical health is profound, and your work will simply not get done until you have dealt with the crisis.

"When the mind suffers the body cries out".

Edson

I worked in the finance industry some for two decades, and spent time with a very successful man who worked in the field of consolidating debt. Now we would call it the sub-prime finance market. He said something that is relevant here. In all the time he had spent in the sector, he had never met anyone who had money worries, he had only ever met people with a lack of money worries.

I am told casinos give people chips to bet with because it does not feel like money. Credit and debit cards are similar; you don't feel like you're spending money, until it's too late.

"There is no dignity quite so impressive, and no independence quite so important, as living within your means."

Calvin Coolidge

When you fail to budget, you will run into financial problems. This can completely derail your time at university. It can in fact bring it to a premature end.

Aldi and Lidl have supermarkets in many university towns. This is not coincidence. They are good for shoppers who have a limited budget. They're referred to as "limited range discounters" by the larger supermarket chains. You are of course free to shop wherever and whenever you want but planning and organising this will offer significant benefits.

Many Sandwich shops sell off their stock close to the end of the day. It's better than throwing it away. Bargains can be picked up.

Many supermarkets sell off items at heavily reduced prices at certain times of the day. It's very easy to find out which local supermarkets do this, and when. It can stretch your food budget significantly.

Use a basket not a trolley. It becomes heavy quite quickly, which limits the time you spend shopping. Trolleys have a much larger capacity, don't involve you carrying anything, and this encourages you to stay longer, spend more, and that includes impulse purchases.

Remember that you have limited storage where you live. Stocking up probably won't help you, and will not help with budgeting, particularly if items go out of date and have to be thrown away.

"Don't go shopping when you're hungry" is good advice. It means we don't plan, or budget, we buy what we're going to eat there and then. Expensive, including some poor choices, not part of a balanced diet. Plan your shopping, you will have time.

Shopping is seen as a chore. It's certainly not cool, and not something you would talk about doing, or having done. Being hungry and broke isn't a good look. Option a) or option b) it's up to you.

Fantastic Plastic, or is it??

Money, or sometimes the lack of it, plays a huge part in our lives. When you are at university this is thrown into sharp relief. We want to have fun and enjoy the adventure. Perfectly reasonable and understandable. We don't want to be stuck in halls when everyone else seems to be living the high life.

I am devoting a chapter to the topic of credit cards, their advantages and disadvantages. Credit card debt can be compared to Hampton Court maze. Very easy to get into, but getting out is a different proposition entirely. Problems with credit card debt will follow you long after your time at university has ended.

Credit cards are now everywhere. They are ubiquitous. They are pushed, and the offers are taken up every day. Paying by credit card is synonymous with ease and convenience. A tap of the credit card and the deal is done. Instant, painless and both easier and safer than carrying cash. When you open a student bank account you may well be offered a credit card by the bank.

This chapter is not intended to look at any/every credit card in detail. The purpose to explain how they work and highlight potential pitfalls and problems.

When we are away from home for the first time, we start to make decisions independently. It doesn't mean that because we are making them, that we have the understanding/experience required to make good ones!! However, good or bad, we deal with/live with the consequences of every decision we make. That's how life works, not just life at university.

At this point I think it is fair to suggest that credit cards can be described in the same way as the relationship some people have with alcohol; it is a good slave but a bad master. Credit cards are things you must control, or they will most decidedly control you, and curtail your financial freedom.

How do they work? Your credit card bill is made up of capital and interest.

1) When you buy using a card, the payment is made on your behalf to the retailer by the credit card company.
2) The payment appears on your next statement as debt you owe.
3) You are then required to make a payment. Three options:
   a) Pay the full balance.
   b) Make the minimum payment.
   c) Make a payment which is more than the minimum payment but less than the full balance.

The credit card issuer charges interest on the outstanding balance on a monthly basis. This means your indebtedness is increasing if you have any balance outstanding. Part of every monthly payment you make goes to paying interest, and the rest to reducing the debt, or the outstanding balance.

Please click on the link below to see how serious your situation can become, and how many years it can take you to get out of the hole you find yourself in.

<u>Credit card minimum repayment calculator - Money Saving Expert</u>

By managing credit cards skilfully, you can make purchases, and pay up to 56 days later without paying any interest. This involves you making the purchase on the first day after the last credit card statement was issued, and you then pay the full balance the last moment the payment is due. This requires self-control and effective financial management. It is the extreme example. Most people couldn't make every purchase on day 1 and pay on day 56. It is for illustrative purposes only. What can happen next? We don't pay the full balance, we pay the minimum, and the bill starts to grow.

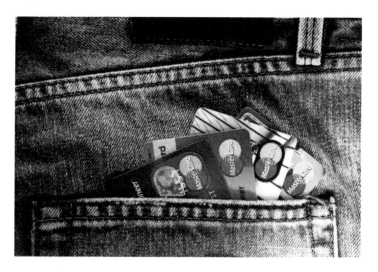

Some Advantages of credit cards

1) Convenience. Online purchases rely on customers using their plastic.

2) Equal liability. I worked in the finance industry for twenty years; more specifically, consumer finance. I know how the sausages are made!! There is comprehensive legislation covering all areas of lending. One such piece of legislation is The Consumer Credit Act 1974. This is something it is very important to know about, well beyond your time at university. It is extremely valuable information if you find yourself in dispute

with a retailer, or they have gone out of business.

Section 75 of the Consumer Credit Act - Which?

According to section 75 the credit card company is as liable for goods and/ services purchased by you using your credit card as the retailer/supplier is. Minimum cost of the goods/services is £100 and the maximum cost is £30,000. The reality is that if the retailer is no longer in business you are in a much better position than someone who has paid using another method.

It is important to note this does not apply to debit cards or charge cards, it is limited to credit cards. It also applies to other forms of consumer lending but my focus in this chapter is on credit cards. This doesn't seem relevant to you at this point. Please bear it in mind when you have travelled abroad, and as we see on the news on a regular basis, you find yourself stuck. Having your credit card company on your side can make the difference between a nightmare scenario, and slight inconvenience whist they solve the problem for you.

3) Safer and more secure than cash.
4) Easier to keep a record of your spending.
5) You Can manage without cash in lots of circumstances. Standing at an ATM late at night is not really a good idea.
6) We are now moving increasingly to a payment system where retailers do not accept cash. Without a credit/debit card option, you are excluded.

Some disadvantages of credit cards

1) Failing to manage the card properly. There are a number of options when the time comes to pay.

Options for payment

a) You use the card for ease and convenience. You pay off your outstanding balance every month. Great!!

How does the credit card issuer make money when you do this? They do not rely on your interest charges for their income. They charge businesses for the privilege of having a credit card facility. Every purchase represents a cost to the retailer.

b) You do not pay it all off. Over time this debt can build into what is referred to as a hard-core balance. The clue's in the description.

At this point you are aiming to service a debt. Now things can get ugly in a hurry.

2) <u>You continue to use the card, and increase your level of debt.</u>

The debt then grows and the interest payments get larger. Note: interest payments, not payments which will reduce and then clear the debt. You may find the credit card company will increase your credit limit. Guess what happens next? … Correct!!

3) <u>Repayments can get larger unless you reduce or pay off the balance.</u>
4) <u>Impulse purchases.</u> It is very easy to tap the card or click "move to checkout" or "confirm and pay" without thinking. It's harder to part with cold hard cash than tap and forget.
5) <u>Signing up for another credit card</u>

There is now an industry within an industry, offering balance transfer. You move the debt to another credit card company in return for an interest free period. The people who take advantage of this were referred to as "debt tramps." They're certainly in a debt trap.

There is now another industry within an industry, which is debt consolidation. They roll your debts up together into a loan, and this can reduce your monthly outgoings. Three things happen:

1) The debt is transferred to another lender.
2) They charge you interest.
3) The debt takes a significant length of time to pay off. You continue to pay interest.

Hopefully, this has highlighted how the problem can get worse and more expensive over time. The financial burden gets heavier. The existence of the problem causes worry and stress, and they are not going to help you as you navigate life at university. Stress can also have a physical side.

When the mind is in pain the body cries out.

As with many other things, the problem of credit card debt sneaks up on you. Before you know what's happening, you are down the rabbit hole.

Credit worthiness is now more important than ever. Without a good credit rating, it can be difficult to rent or buy a flat or apartment. Unless you keep your credit card payments up to date, you will be regarded as being in default, and that will work against you when you are trying to rent or obtain any form of credit.

Final thought on credit cards, debit cards, and charge cards, if you have them. Fraud is a huge problem in the financial sector. It is possible to have your cards cloned without you even knowing about it until it's too late, and you have lost money.

Fraudsters use Radio frequency identification (RFID) to clone your cards. It would make a great deal of sense to buy and use an RFID blocking wallet or purse.

Preventing the fraudsters succeeding is far easier than trying to sort the aftermath.

Looking after your mental health

You are now living independently, very often for the first time in your life. You can make all your own decisions. You have control. You may have chosen your university in part because it is a long way from home. It adds to the feeling of being a student.

We are now more aware than ever before of the importance of mental health, and the ways in which it can be harmed. It can be harmed before we realise it, and prevention is most definitely better than cure.

Problems with mental health can sneak up on you. It is like gaining weight. You do not realise your body weight has increased until an item of clothing that previously fitted perfectly is suddenly too tight. Look out for the warning signs that your mental health is being compromised. There are many forms of mental health issues including depression, anxiety, OCD and panic disorders. This is not a complete list. They all have symptoms you can identify, if you are alert to the warning signs.

*1 in 4 university students experience mental health difficulties each year

**There is a scientifically proven link between high IQ and problems with mental health

The universities all have support systems in place, but they are only ever useful if you access them!! You are making a huge change in your life. It will present challenges. You must be alert to the warning signs that your mental health is being compromised.

A difficulty or disorder can attack you without warning, and everyone can be a victim. You are not immune, but you can guard against it. Your mental strength is a huge benefit when you are facing setbacks and reversals. It is very precious. Protect and value it every day of your life.

Work on the principle of; if in doubt, seek help immediately. There is sometimes a feeling of shame associated with mental health issues, but it is most important you get past it. Reach out for help and you will receive it, every time!! You will never be judged or ridiculed when you ask for help. Your friends will support you, and if they don't, they aren't fit to be your friends, because they definitely aren't. That is not a casual comment, it is deadly serious.

* Source: <u>One in four students suffer from mental health problems | YouGov</u>

** Source: <u>Having a High IQ May Lead to Increased Risk of Mental Illness | Thriveworks</u>

Warning signs can include:

- Problems sleeping
- Problems with anger
- Paranoia
- Excessive mood swings
- Dependence on alcohol/drugs
- Struggling to concentrate
- Suicidal thoughts
- Loss of appetite/binge eating
- Not wanting to get out of bed
- Not wanting to get dressed when you get out of bed.
- Having no interest in things. Lack of motivation. It becomes more of an effort to do things, and later to do even small things.
- Going out with friends is too much of an effort.
- Confusion
- Withdrawal

This is not intended to be a complete list

Do not suffer in silence to impress or fool people. You are never alone, even when you are on your own. Every university has a comprehensive support system. The help you need is always there. Having a bad day or feeling isolated is fairly typical in life generally. Everyone has this type of experience.

However, if you continue to feel like this, do something about it. Speak to someone. You are not alone, even if you feel alone. We can all feel overwhelmed at times. Help and support is only ever a click, or a telephone call away, 24/7!! There are many sources of help available.

One very well-known source of help:

The Samaritans. Tel: 116 123 Free call. E-mail: jo@samaritans.org

Points to ponder:

"The only mistake you can make is not asking for help."

Sandeep Jauhar

"Asking for help isn't weak, it's a great example of how to take care of yourself."

Charlie Brown

Sometimes you feel completely isolated. Your campus feels like this,

Even if it looks like this!!

Its ok not to be ok, it really is!!

What's not ok is doing nothing about it!!

The actor Arnold Schwarzenegger said that a tactic to succeed is to fake it till you make it. Present yourself in the way you would present yourself when you have become a success. This can perhaps be described as bluffing, putting on a front. Many students are bluffing, the only difference is they are better at it than you are, and they have managed to conceal their feelings, which may be exactly the same as yours.

Not everyone who appears to be the life and soul of the party is what they appear to be. Never judge yourself based on what you know about others, or importantly, what you **think** you know about others. The truth is you don't know about others, you think you know, based solely on the way they present themselves.

To use another example from casinos, it is said that successful poker players succeed because they play the people, not the cards. Bluffing is something we all do, to some extent. Do not try so hard that you start to fool yourself and play a role. When you feel you need help, please reach out.

You must not overlook your physical health.

You will need a GP. Ask at the university about temporary registration. You should not register as a permanent patient. You can only register with one GP. It could mean you may have to travel hundreds of miles to see your GP in the future.

Before you dismiss this suggestion, google fresher's flu!!

Dr. Google is not your friend!!

It is very easy to google anything now. I used to tell my students how to do different types of research. No the case anymore. Everything we want or need to know is a google away.

When you think you have an ailment or illness, go to see a medical professional. You are responsible for your own health and wellbeing. When you do not feel well, do not disregard or ignore warning signs, when you feel you have a health problem. A practical guide is to put safety first as your version of first aid. You are living independently, so you will be facing situations which are new to you. The university pastoral system can point you the right way.

When you google your symptoms, you will not be able to give all the information needed for diagnosis. You're not a medical professional, you don't know what to look for. Therefore, you will then frighten yourself when you read about what could actually be wrong with you.

I say again, please see medical professional. Something to think about in advance; please don't go clutching a printed page of symptoms from google. The person you are seeing has a medical degree and possibly decades of experience. You have half an idea, an iPad and a printer!! In the annals of medicine, no doctor has ever taken a printed page from a patient and said, "wow, I didn't know that!! You know more than I do about your symptoms. Well done."

Don't scare yourself. Go and be reassured and/or treated.

Avoiding changing your dentist would make sense. You can arrange appointments when you are home.

Diet is important. Poor diet is proven to damage both your physical and mental health.

Diet and Mental Health Connection - How Foods Affects Mental Health (paleohacks.com)

As a general rule, try to avoid heavily processed foods. They are convenient, but you should limit the intake. It's easy to buy a takeaway or visit a fast-food outlet. It's quick, convenient, expensive, and can cause long-term harm if you continue to eat this way.

Think about a balance as well as a budget. A healthy diet can often include some convenience foods. Learn to cook the basics. One of the recommendations to help deal with clinical depression is to have a healthy diet.

Another is to take exercise. Look after yourself, mentally and physically. You must decide what exercise means to you, and what diet means to you, but be objective and sensible. You're taking responsibility for every part of your life; treat yourself and your mental and physical health with care; respect and value them.

We have looked at planning. This should include times when you're doing absolutely no university work of any kind. Discipline yourself to using time each week to get way, take exercise, be tranquil, do things that make you feel glad to be alive. University isn't supposed to take over your life!!

Every university has a wide range of clubs, groups, and societies. They offer a great opportunity to meet people as well as having and sharing new experiences. You can recharge your batteries and grow as a person.

The writer Phil Redmond described watching television as a second-choice activity. He says you flop down in front of it until you find something better to do. You are at an incredibly exciting time in your life, you will always be able to find something better to do. Be mindful that too much is definitely too much!! Balance is good.

I wouldn't behave like that!!

when we live independently or alone, there is an inherent danger in place. Everything we do or think is acceptable as far as we're concerned, because there is nobody to help correct your course of action. You will not think your actions are wrong. We would not choose to do something we think is wrong or bad, we have a moral compass. However, we are the arbiter of our own actions. It can continue to take us down a wrong path. Allied to any ongoing struggles with mental health, the results can be disastrous, and recovery can take a long time, or may tragically, prove to be impossible.

There is a temptation as humans, to overestimate our ability to deal with new situations. This is particularly so when we are young, and on the threshold of life, waiting to see what new experiences we will have, and how great they will be. We have all been there. You believe you are invincible and invulnerable. You are the superhero waiting to be discovered, Superman or

Superwoman, a Superboy or Supergirl, capable of achieving anything.

When we are in a safe, nurturing environment, we can develop and grow, becoming stronger and better every day. We are making small adjustments when we discover errors, and the journey continues without any significant interruption or drama.

Circadian rhythms, also known as the body clock, need to be understood in detail when we have made a huge change in our lives.

Human bodies work very efficiently, and often without us being aware of what is happening. When we change our environment, we can find ourselves out of balance. During breakfast in the restaurant of hotels all over the world, the same question is asked; "How did you sleep?" "Not very well, I can't sleep in a strange bed."

Think of this in terms, not of a couple of nights at a business conference, but your life for the next three years!!

Sleep is a vital part of the human cycle of wellbeing. Unless we have a sleep pattern that meets our needs, we suffer badly, and there can be long term negative consequences.

Effects of problems with sleeping properly can include memory problems, increased body weight, and mood swings. Memory problems and lectures do not make good bedfellows, please excuse the pun!! It will detract from the value of all activities involving the need to absorb and remember key details. In a place of education this must be avoided if you are to gain the maximum benefit from your investment of both time and money.

As with many aspects of the human condition, we only realise there is a problem when there are signs and symptoms, we do not seem to be able to anticipate problems, and head them off. We're dealing with things when the symptoms are already established.

There is a huge adjustment to be made at this point. Literally everything has changed. The word "literally" is often misused, but in this case it's accurate. Nothing is the same; where you live, who you live with, where you spend your days, where you spend your free time, what you do, every single day. Your world has been turned upside down, and that will, and does, present you with challenges.

At this point, we have to accept that our invincibility chip may have a flaw. We are all unique, which is priceless, but we share a great many similarities. People buy lottery tickets every week, with odds of 14,000,000 to 1 against you winning. They say, "somebody has to win, it could be me." They continue with this behaviour for years, spending hundreds, if not thousands, of pounds.

They establish a pattern of behaviour which means they buy tickets at certain times, to ensure they're not too late for particular draw. Owners of small shops were prepared to pay to have a lottery ticket facility installed, because they knew the customers who come in to buy lottery tickets would make other, impulse purchases, which made the investment in the lottery ticket facility a lucrative one.

No evaluation of the odds, or alternative use of the hundreds or thousands of pounds, will ever take place. They believe they may eventually win. "You've got to be in it to win it" is what they say. True, undeniably true. But you wouldn't bet on anything else at odds of 14,000,000 to 1. We believe, so we abandon the need for, or value of, logical thought.

We also apply the exact opposite way of thinking in other circumstances. We take foolish, unnecessary, and dangerous risks. We ignore warning signs and health and safety advice. "It won't happen to me, I'll be ok" is what people say, and believe. Committed smokers apply this logic. "My grandfather smoked all his life , and he lived until he was 88!!" I'm sure that's true. Two things; you're not your grandfather, and perhaps if he hadn't smoked he would have lived even longer.

This unpreparedness to apply logic and reason to situations, is a basic human flaw. We believe what we want to believe. We double down when we are challenged.

This is originally a term used in gambling, meaning you double a bet. We restate our argument and ignore or reject alternatives. People respond using this strategy when asked about their purchase of lottery tickets. They would point out that; "somebody won £10,000,0000 only last week." You're not going to convince them their strategy is flawed. Incredibly graphic images on cigarette packets do not deter determined smokers. "It won't happen to me." An even more nihilistic approach is to say, "you've got to die of something." That casual, flippant argument only works until you realise you've shortened your own life.

People don't take advice. If they did, far fewer people, would be overweight, have problems with drugs or alcohol, break the law, or wreck their own lives with a combination of tragic, unforced errors.

This phenomenon is explored in depth in an excellent article written by Elizabeth Kolbert. It is inciteful and particularly well written.

<u>Why Facts Don't Change Our Minds | The New Yorker</u>

"The Stanford studies became famous. Coming from a group of academics in the nineteen-seventies, the contention that people can't think straight was shocking. It isn't any longer. Thousands of subsequent experiments have confirmed (and elaborated on) this finding."

Elizabeth Colbert

When we live independently, and/or alone, and have nobody to challenge our opinions or rationalise with us, it has the potential to be/become a big problem.

The purpose of this chapter is not to ask you to ignore thousands of years of human evolution, it is simply to make you aware of the fact it exists. The phenomenon known as "confirmation bias" encourages us to ignore facts that contradict our own beliefs. Please be aware that no human is omnipotent. Have a look through the other end of the telescope. Looking at decisions we make more objectively helps eliminate errors that have long term negative consequences. That this is something of which you need to be aware.

AI, education, and the future

There is a huge amount written and said about AI, from articles saying it will be catastrophic for all of humanity, to proof that it is aiding mankind in shaping a new and much better future in areas such as medical research. When there has been any groundbreaking development, there will be a wide range of reactions, both positive and negative. When radio became popular, it was suggested it would mean the death of the theatre. When TV came along, it would be the end of radio and theatre. The predictions were unfounded. Theatre, radio and TV all peacefully co-exist. They still have their place in our lives, and have not been rendered obsolete by new developments.

Chat GPT, machine learning, and AI in other forms is here to stay and will grow at a phenomenal rate. There is now a 2D avatar, created by AI, with a record deal provided by a global label, and it is also a significant social media influencer. It doesn't mean humans will stop making records. It will take its place alongside them. It doesn't mean human influencers will suddenly give up and go in another career direction. Why would they? Did the first ever influencer give up when others arrived?? Of course not!! Cars haven't stopped people riding bicycles, or travelling on buses or trains. They fit together to form a more complex pattern of travel options.

The ultimate measure of how you spent your time at university is your degree classification. This, in turn, is measured by the work you produce and submit. That in turn is a measure of your understanding of the subject you are studying. AI will become integral to all places of learning, how can it not?? However, it is there to help you, not to do the work for you.

The advent of e-mail, and a range of intranet packages introduced in places of learning, have replaced the old ways of submitting work. No longer do we wait patiently whilst the printers produce dozens of pages for us, which we then organise, prepare and deliver. What had taken hours and hours is now done, literally, by pressing a button.

The "send" button has replaced a great deal of effort and leg work. What you send is the key. It has to reach the standard, as it had to in the old system of delivery. You are there to increase and improve your subject knowledge, not try to find a way to make machine learning do all the work for you. Remember, your knowledge will be evaluated. AI is a tool in a comprehensive and varied academic toolbox. Use the right tool, in the right, way, to do the right job.

AI will, undoubtedly, be able to answer your questions. That's not the key to your success.

The keys are knowing what questions to ask, and being able to explain and describe the work you have submitted, when asked.

We all have our own writing style, and a level of vocabulary we typically use. To submit work that bears no relation to these factors is the first indicator that all is not as it should be.

It is possible to copy text written in a language we don't speak or understand, absolutely perfectly. We have learned nothing, and aside from practising our keyboard skills, have gained nothing.

The whole purpose of going to university to study your chosen subject in detail over three years, and your degree provides unambiguous confirmation that we have the achieved requisite level of knowledge and understanding. AI will be a tool to help you, nothing more. Understanding and interpretation of researched data and information is how we develop our knowledge. Find it where you choose to, but understand it, and please don't believe a "copy and paste" of AI generated information will get you there.

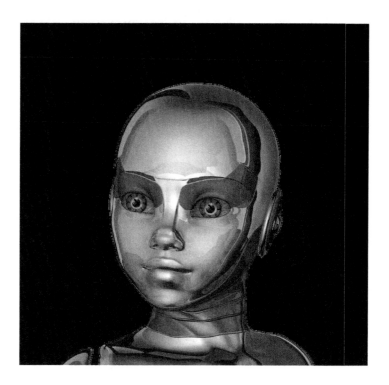

Nobody can accurately foretell the future. There are many who believe in horoscopes, or similar ways to predict the future, but we can't do it with any degree of accuracy.

Certain things come along that are so incredible, they genuinely change the way we live and work. They were not predicted, they are the product of out of the box thinking and amazing leaps of the imagination that allowed a tiny percentage of people to influence the global population every day of their lives.

The arrival of the train, following the success of Stephenson's Rocket at the Rainhill Trials, allowed people to experience things they had never even dreamed about before. A trip to the seaside became possible, as did holidays in places you had never even heard of. Businesses could develop new markets, and products could be moved over distances not previously dreamed possible. Local became regional, and regional became national, before becoming international.

When Alexander Graham Bell invented the telephone, it led to the way people communicated changing forever. The world was suddenly not a collection of remote places, but the beginning of an interconnected network of countries, people and businesses.

The invention of the internal combustion engine allowed independent travel, and the family car eventually became a staple in many homes. Entrepreneurs could use vans and commercial vehicles to build and develop their businesses.

When Wilbur and Orville Wright took to the sky in Kittyhawk, North Carolina, air travel was born, and the world shrank in size. We could travel around the globe, to seek new opportunities, and to be reunited with loved ones. Package holidays depended, and still depend on, cost effective air travel. Their father, Bishop Milton Wright had famously said, "men will never fly because flying is reserved for the Angels."

When Clive Sinclair introduced the pocket calculator, it had the most incredible effect. Suddenly, the way calculations were made changed. You could carry the technology with you. Mental arithmetic became unimportant to the point of becoming irrelevant. Students changed the way they studied maths because they had a new tool to help. It was a seminal moment in business and education. They are now so ubiquitous, they're built into every mobile telephone.

When Tim Berners-Lee created the internet, it was so incredible it changed everything we could do, quite literally. We are now so interconnected, we cannot imagine a time when we were not plugged in. "What's the Wi-Fi password?" is one of the first questions people ask in new locations. It's often written down, to make the question irrelevant.

These examples of great leaps forward were embraced globally and have changed both what we do and how we do it, including communication, work, travel, leisure, and education.

The introduction and exponential growth of IA is on a par with these advances.

The next chapter
of your life

You've graduated!! Well done. Now get ready for several things to happen very quickly. You'll be moving to new accommodation, if you were staying in halls, or renting near the university. That's quite an upheaval. Moving back home will perhaps not be as straightforward as you think, adjustments will need to be made.

I am keen to highlight things which are ongoing. You will be asked a number of searching questions, all in quick succession, and they can be annoying, even if the person asking has the best of intentions.

At this point, you may have to deal with the upheaval of changing where you are living and adjusting to a new way of organising your life, which is exactly what you did when you went to university in the first place!!

Question one: What is your degree in?

Question two: (Optional) what does that involve?

Question three: What are you going to do next?

It is worth noting that, depending on your answer to question three, you will, almost certainly, be offered advice. You have not asked for advice, or people's opinions, or guidance, or insights, you have simply answered a question. Usually, their sentence starts with the words, "if I were you" or, "in your position I would" or; "If you'll take my advice" or, "you'll have to get a job" or similar. However, you're not me, are you? you're not in my position, I didn't ask for your advice, no, I don't have to get a job. Those responses are better said silently to yourself, but the sentiment is the key.

Nobody is in your position because nobody else is you. Several additional questions will pop into your head, which you may choose not to articulate. What's it got to do with you? Why do you think you're equipped to advise me? Why do you think I want your advice? What are you basing your advice on?

During your time at university, you have lived in a bubble. Almost everybody you met, or interacted with, was involved in or with your university. For MPs and other people involved in politics the UK, there is a thing called the Westminster Bubble, which is the environment in which they all work, and sometimes, live and work. They are detached from the world the rest of us occupy and function in, and therefore have no understanding of what I will choose to call the outside world, for the purpose of demonstrating this phenomenon.

There is a similar situation in the EU, which is known as the "Brussels Bubble." Such bubbles mean interaction with people or groups from outside the bubble is limited. It means your perspective is influenced as a result. It has been said that a person is the sum of the five people they spend most of their time with. Outside your bubble, in the real world, people are from a wide variety of social groups, with a huge variation in personality types and behavioural characteristics.

Some people will admire you because you are a graduate, some people will resent or envy you because you're a graduate. Some people will want to build you up, and some to put you down. Every action a human being takes is chosen with a purpose in mind; sometimes vital and sometimes trivial. Remember this when people interact with you. Anything they say or do has a purpose.

When you leave the university bubble, your world changes, and, fairly soon afterwards, your world view will change.

A quote from a character in a very famous book can be your guide, here.

"No matter what anyone else says to you, don't let 'em get your goat".

Atticus Finch

To Kill a Mockingbird

Alternatively, we can take another view, and make sure we don't have to think; "that sounded better in my head," after you have said it out loud.

However, they usually haven't been to university, and therefore have no frame of reference. They see student debt as something of a millstone because debt is bad. Looking through a different lens, they usually have a mortgage and a car payment to make each month. Perception is everything. You don't have to pay your loan off as quickly as possible, any more than they have to pay their mortgage off as quickly as possible. It has its advantages, but it should not be the solitary, or even predominant, focus. They cannot say what they would do in your position, because they would not have taken on debt to go to university in the first place. Your investment of time and money has opened doors they cannot expect or aspire to ever step through themselves.

As you planned your journey to, and your time at, university, so you should plan the next step. "All good things come to an end" it is said, possibly to be replaced by something better and even more exciting.

In my long experience, people don't take advice, they simply don't!! They may appear to be listening, but that's as far as it goes.

So rather than call this chapter, or indeed any part of this book, a source of advice, I'm going to describe it as a way in which I will share thoughts and ideas. Lots of people will offer you advice. Some of them will be well meaning. Sometimes, the advice is very valuable, sometimes; less so!! Almost never could it be categorised as expert advice.

We do not go through life unaided or unsupported, it's not possible. However, we often take on board only what we like to hear and ignore the rest. What we like to hear may not be what we should hear or need to hear.

On that basis, let's lay out some options that may be placed before you, prior to waving goodbye to your time as an undergraduate.

Your university will have a comprehensive system in place to look at next steps with you. Please take the time to explore options with them. This is something to consider as you approach the end of your time at university, it's not something to devote time to at an earlier stage. As you approach the completion of your time as an undergraduate, you will have sufficient time to evaluate options, and move forward.

It's a choice you should consider carefully. Doing nothing is a choice. In the words of a famous song.

"If you choose not to decide, you still have made a choice."

"Freewill" by Rush

They are not mutually exclusive. I have not presented options using headings as crude as advantages and disadvantages. They are, after all, rather subjective in nature. Rather, there are some points to ponder in respect of each one. Additionally, the "other" option on the list is equally important. This is not an exhaustive list, it is only a compilation of some popular choices.

"Other" may be perfect to for you, even though you may not know what "other" looks like until you start the search. There will be other considerations in respect of all options which are personal to you and therefore, could never be included. The purpose is to help with evaluating options, not to give advice, or produce a list including every possible factor to be considered. It would be astonishingly arrogant of me to suggest I can advise people I have never met or spoken to. My objective is to share thoughts and ideas, which, I hope very sincerely, will help you generate your own thoughts and ideas.

There are lots of routes to take, and it's important to remember you can double back, or change direction. You're not on rails, without the ability to change direction. Your life; your decisions. Mistakes are learning opportunities, and they all provide us with knowledge and insight, even the more serious ones.

"That which harms, instructs."

Benjamin Franklin

I'm not for one moment suggesting you should be reckless or careless or have no regard for the consequences of your actions.

You will never go anywhere, or experience anything, if you don't decide and go with it. As you stay still, the world around you changes and evolves, even though you may not notice.

Take the time you need to make decisions. Remember, you're the only one who has to deal with the consequences. Other people have their idea about what your timetable should be. It's your timetable!! You're also the only one to reap the benefits that have accrued. A group of people can go on holiday together and have different experiences and contrasting memories. The experience is as individual and unique as you are.

We must own our actions, and their outcomes. We make decisions we think are good, based on the information available at the time. We also make rash or poor decision, on the spur of the moment, or because we are led by others. "That one's on me" is hard to say but makes you a truly unusual person. So many people play the blame game. It stops personal growth, limits your self-belief, and ultimately, the quality and value of your life. People make mistakes and get things wrong. It's how we learn and grow; but only if we learn from or mistakes. "I won't do that again."

During your adult life you may go down a number of roads. Gone are the days when a person found a job, and stayed there until retirement, possibly without even a promotion in all that time. As you travel, please remember you can go in any direction, and you can also retrace your steps, or change direction, at will. When something doesn't work for you, make a change. Please remember a bad day, or a couple of bad days, doesn't mean it's a bad choice. You will know when you need to make a change. It may be that option will still work for you, but at a later date. "Never say never again" to borrow a famous film title.

Some options include;

Study for a Master's Degree

There will be a significant additional cost, although there may well be a reduced cost if you stay with the same university. You will no doubt have a better understanding of your chosen subject. You will perhaps be looking at changed career opportunities, but you should remember that your commercial experience, which employers may like to see, will be limited. It will take you no time to adjust to your surroundings as you continue with your studies, and the challenges you face should be, for the most part, only be academic in nature. You already have an established structure to your life at university.

Travelling

Exciting alternative to many of the other options listed. You can see the world and, have an adventure. There will certainly be a cost, and travel should be planned carefully, having regard to political situations and potential dangers in parts of the world with which you are unfamiliar. Graduates often describe this as their opportunity to find themselves. There may well be opportunities to gain teaching experience whilst travelling. Teaching English as a foreign language (TEFL) is popular, and there may be other teaching opportunities available. It can help fund your travelling, and will be a valuable addition to your CV, and perhaps, provide clues as to your future employment options.

Volunteering

A useful way to gain work experience, at the same time as making a valuable contribution to your local community, and help others. It will be unpaid, but you can work in a way, and at a time, that suits your needs. It will enhance your CV and add to your employability. It has long been said, and it is still true, that you are better placed looking for a job when you're in a job.

Internship

Great way to gain experience, either in your chosen are of interest, or to better understand the world of work in more general terms. It will be unpaid, and there is a belief that, in some situations, you are providing free labour, and as such, you are being taken advantage of. You will gain valuable experience, which can be added to your CV, and increase your employability, in the future.

It is also a possible way to secure a position with an organisation. Recruiting you is much less risky if you've already worked there for several weeks. The employer has had a chance to try before they buy.

It's a great way to prove yourself and show how you could add value to the organisation.

Employment

This is a path **taken** by a great many people. This is quite distinct from the path **chosen** by people. They are two different things. It is seen as a safe option and can result in a comfortable and less stressful life. It pays a salary and allows you to establish and maintain a lifestyle. The alternative view is that if you work for someone other than yourself, you line their pockets, not yours. You're either working on your dream or your boss's.

Should you go down this road, it is not the simple, easy option it may appear to be. You will be competing for positions. In order to secure the career you want, you must take the recruitment process seriously.

You must prepare and perform to a standard. Employers won't pay you tens of thousands of pounds each year simply because you have a degree. In some circumstances, the fact you have a degree will open the door for you, but what you do when you get through the door is what brings you success, or results in rejection.

We should also consider that where we start, and where we finish, may well be very different places, in many cases. You may alter your career path several times, through promotions, or changes of employer. Be prepared to be flexible, and to recognise and seize opportunities.

"Only a fifth of students believe being articulate is key to employability".

The Telegraph

Compare this with a very famous quote.

"It's not what we don't know that gets us in trouble. It's what we know for sure that just ain't so."

Mark Twain

Please be assured that, being articulate is critical to your success in interviews, and from there to employment. Unless you can articulate your views and responses, you will not be able to persuade any employer to invest in you.

Start your own business.

Not for the faint hearted!! Upsides include complete control over your direction of travel, and the ability to make and implement your decisions.

Downsides can include significant levels of stress, and the need to take financial risks, which may ultimately result in huge losses. Many successful business people have come crashing down, lost everything, started again, and became a huge success. Rags to riches and back again, is a more familiar story than you might think. Entrepreneurs who have lost everything take it further. Rags to riches, back to rags, and on to riches … again!! You're not beaten when you're defeated, you're only beaten when you quit.

I could write a great deal more about this option, including information about company structures and how funding can be obtained and used, about marketing, promotion, cashflow, and unique selling points. However, I will only add one more sentence at this point. Choosing this option will be determined, at the beginning, by two things: your desire to be your own boss, and your appetite for risk. The rest will come later. The desire to succeed must be greater than the fear of failure, if this is a choice you pursue.

There is a great deal of support available for entrepreneurs who are prepared to take the risk, and it can be accessed with only a few clicks. Groups of like-minded people can be found on forums, and through professional organisations.

Download a business plan template to help you evaluate this. It won't answer all your questions, but it may prompt you to ask some you hadn't perhaps considered. Do not rush in, take the time you need to make a series of decisions that all lead you to decide if it's right for you.

Other

Limited only by your imagination!!

We live in an interconnected world, a global community. Opportunities exist now that weren't even dreamed about only twenty years ago. They way we live and work is unimaginably different from two decades ago. You can live on one continent, and work on another, all from the comfort of a sun lounger!! Dare to dream, and then dare to turn it into your reality, whatever it is!!

Over to you

We have reached the final chapter of the book. You are going to start writing your own chapters to complete your own book. It will be unique to you.

You are driving the car that is your university journey. Steer it wisely and safely.

Shoulda, woulda, coulda

Words tinged with bitterness and regret. Please don't let the story of your university journey end with one or more of these words. Nobody is in control of what you do or don't do, except you. When people ask about your time at university, please make sure your response doesn't include one of these words, they're incredibly telling, but by the time you're using them it's already too late to make the most of your time at university............ it's behind you.

Make your achievement something to sing out loud about!!!

Final point to ponder:

"The problem with youth is it's wasted on the young".

George Bernard Shaw

Be the exception. Don't waste yours, invest some of it in your future self!!

Follow our QR Code to gain access to all the links
from this book and download/view a free e-copy.

Printed in Great Britain
by Amazon

31622515R00066